salmonpoetry

Diverse Voices from Ireland and the World

ALSO BY KEVIN HIGGINS

POETRY COLLECTIONS

The Boy with No Face (Salmon Poetry, 2005)

Time Gentlemen, Please (Salmon Poetry, 2008)

Frightening New Furniture (Salmon Poetry, 2010)

The Ghost in the Lobby (Salmon Poetry, 2014)

Song of Songs 2.0 (Salmon Poetry, 2017)

Sex and Death at Merlin Park Hospital (Salmon Poetry, 2019)

The Colour Yellow & The Number 19: Negative Thoughts That Helped One Man Mostly Retain His Sanity During 2020 (Nuascealta, 2020)

Ecstatic (Salmon Poetry, 2022)

ESSAYS

Mentioning the War: Essays & Reviews 1999-2011 (Salmon Poetry, 2012)

'Thrills & Difficulties: Being A Marxist Poet In 21st Century Ireland' (Beir Bua Press, 2021)

Life Itself

KEVIN HIGGINS

Edited by
Susan Millar DuMars

Published in 2025 by
Salmon Poetry
Cliffs of Moher, County Clare, Ireland
Website: www.salmonpoetry.com
Email: info@salmonpoetry.com

Copyright © The estate of Kevin Higgins, 2025

ISBN 978-1-915022-63-9

All rights reserved. No part of this publication may be reproduced or transmitted in any form or by any means, electronic or mechanical, including photography, recording, or any information storage or retrieval system, without permission in writing from the publisher. The book is sold subject to the condition that it shall not, by way of trade or otherwise, be lent, resold or otherwise circulated without the publisher's prior consent in any form of binding or cover other than that in which it is published and without a similar condition, including this condition, being imposed on the subsequent purchaser.

Cover Image: Photo of the author. Photographer unknown.
Cover Design & Typesetting: Siobhán Hutson Jeanotte

Printed in Ireland by Sprint Print

Salmon Poetry gratefully acknowledges the support of
The Arts Council / An Chomhairle Ealaíon

This book is dedicated to everyone working on Claddagh Ward, University College Hospital, Galway

Contents

Introduction 11

i. I Always Thought I'd Live

Life, Death and the Bit In the Middle 17
Check-up 18
To Stability 19
Mostly 20
The Ancestors 21
The Man in Room Fourteen 22
Mr Cogito Considers the Side Effects 23
When I'm Allowed Leave the Cancer Ward 24
On Being Detained At a Medical Facility
   Four Minutes From Your Own Home 26
New Reduced Kevin Higgins 28
Any News? 29
On My Deathbed 30
The Haunting 31
The After Life 32
I Always Thought I'd Live

ii. Waiting for World Peace

This is Not a Well-Made Poem 37
Congratulations 38
Facebook Update 40
Black Notebook, Page 57 41
Irish Literary Society, 2022 42
Critique 43
Note to Self, Re: Evils of Hipster Careerism in the Literary Arts ... 45
For All You Know 46
My Permanent Residence 48
The Visitor 49
Brief Reflection on Not Alienating One's Peers 50
Brief Reflection on Hitler 51
The Meaning 52
Downstairs 54
Ballad of the Crank 55

A Life Disappointed	57
According to Our Intelligence Reports	58
The Secret Life	59
Apartment 5E	60
Things He Isn't Paid to Remember	61
To the Man Who Lost His Shadow	62
I Will Survive	63
Sketch of Mr and Mrs Past Tense	65
Common Sense Climbed Out of the TV the Other Night	66
Your Days of Total Disdain	67
Anxiety Prayer	68
Burden Sharing	69
Potential	71
The Joke	72
The Biden Monologues: Day 457	74
To My Friends Who Said Nothing During the Witch Hunting of Ilhan Omar	76
Utopia American Moderates Dream Into Being	77
I Am an American Leftist	78
Fetish in Which I Visit the Early 1950s (USA Style)	79
The Death by Drowning of Twenty Seven Migrants in the English Channel on Wednesday	80
How to Survive Next Winter	81
The Abolition of What's Next	82
The Angry	83
Deliberately Offensive Song	84
The Dialectics of Irish	86
Redefining Ireland	88
She Had, She Thought, A Thousand Things to Say	89
And Now For the Future	90
August 15, 2021	92
It All Depends	93
Cometh the Hour, Cometh the Dame	94
Hell's Most Boring Room	95
White	96
Temple of Electricity	97
Safe to Say	98
After the Defeat	99
The Old Accusation	100
Exercise in Democracy	102
1996	103
Sunday September the 24th, 7.10pm	104
Waiting for World Peace	106

iii. Things You Should Know About Higgins

The Exclusivity Principle	109
My Becoming	110
The Panic of July 1980	111
St Jude's	112
Being Nobody	113
On Being Even Slightly Well Known	114
You Only Know Someone	115
From a certain angle, he is you	116
Memorial to Myself	117
What I Am Not	118
Status Update at 55 ¼	119
Things You Should Know About Higgins	120
My RSVP	122
The Social Whirl	123
A Kind of Love	124
Friday, November 18, 2022	126
Disappointment	127
Acknowledgments	129
About the Author	131

Introduction

Kevin died on a Tuesday in January. The Sunday before, he emailed new drafts of two poems he'd been struggling with to me, for edits. I was with him in hospital all day, but in the evening went home to feed our cat and allow others a turn to visit. I had a look at the poems, made a couple of minor suggestions involving commas, and sent them back. He thanked me, and for the next three hours until I went to bed we kept up a text conversation, covering everything from how much we loved each other to what music we were each listening to. (The Beatles for me, Neil Diamond for him. Comfort music.) The next morning a nurse phoned me at seven to tell me Kevin's condition had deteriorated. I went straight to the hospital, and was with him until he passed away the following day. Those texts were our last normal exchange. And they started with poems.

We met because of poems; I submitted three to *The Burning Bush*, a journal Kevin was starting with Mike Begnal, at the very start of 1999. Our love affair was bookended by January verse.

Kevin was a weirdly prolific poet. We were each other's first editor, and regularly shared work. Usually we did this at the kitchen table, but sometimes in bed and sometimes when we were out for brunch, after the plates had been cleared. I trusted his judgement of my poems and fiction, finding him an astute, insightful and encouraging editor. He trusted me too. But he wrote so much more than me that our regular sessions weren't enough for him. He would sidle up to me at home and say "I may have written a poem," eyes on his shoes as if this was a confession, and I'd promise to read it as soon as I could. After I'd read it he'd hover in the doorway and ask, "Shit?" I'd assure him it wasn't, and he'd come all the way into the room to hear my feedback. He took criticism well and followed up on the majority of my suggestions. If I had no suggestions he'd push me to come up with some; he didn't want me to let him off easy. Second and third drafts usually came the same day (sometimes the same hour) and he would trail after me until I read the newest version.

Once hospitalised, his poetic output grew. All of the poems in this collection are new, written in the past few years. Some have been published individually, or in chapbooks, while others are making their debut here. Many, including nearly all of the first section, were written in University Hospital, Galway. His poems about battling leukemia are heart-scaldingly honest, and I think they are among the best things he ever wrote. I would not say that writing these comforted him. Nor were they part of an effort at building a mythology of self. When people would say of his illness *why you*, he'd shrug and say *why not me?* He took an active interest in the status of other patients on his ward. He discussed Polish poetry with one of his consultants, Dr. Krawczyk, and later dedicated a poem to him. One of Kevin's nurses had a child who had taken classes with Kevin, and he enthusiastically praised their unique poetic voice while their mother searched his arm for an untapped vein. Getting sick did not cause him to turn inward. Raymond Carver once said that his writing became more successful when he stopped thinking of it as self-expression and began instead to think of it as communication. Kevin's goal was always to communicate. *This is what it's like for me, what about you?* I think to him that writing poems was a way of remaining in the conversation.

I assembled the manuscript for this book in hard copy, working with folders of work marked NEW that I found among Kevin's things. The poems I've left out are on subjects he handled better in other poems. In a very few cases, they're on subjects about which I know he changed his mind. I've edited with a light touch; most of the poems had been through several drafts already and were good to go. I've fiddled with punctuation and stanza breaks where I thought they would make his meaning more apparent. I didn't edit for sound because I want you to hear Kevin's voice, not mine. In the whole collection, there are perhaps half a dozen pieces I changed substantially, again for the sake of clarity. There's one, "From a Certain Angle He is You", which I remember the two of us really struggling with. I carried on the struggle alone, and I hope have fixed the few lines that had annoyed us. It's a remarkable poem, nuanced and heartfelt with a twist at the end that is both satisfying and haunting.

His satires often made me laugh out loud. Even those about current events have an enduring relevance; the more things change, the more they stay the same. Kevin's ability to distil his truth into a memorable and devastating turn of phrase was breathtaking. Every week there's another story on the news I know he would've gleefully sunk his teeth into.

Yet of the poems he will now never write, I most grieve for the introspective ones. As well as being witty and sharp, Kevin could access a tender melancholy in his work, wedding strong imagery with an unguarded nature. Some of the more personal poems in this collection have a tremendous maturity to them, an ability to grapple with paradox that I find very moving. One such poem is "Status Update at 55 ¼". I know I must've read this poem while Kevin was alive, yet I was somehow unprepared for its gut punch ending. Then of course there are the hospital poems, and the piece about his dad ("Friday November 18th, 2022"). In these I see my best friend, the man I loved and the man he was becoming. I will always wonder where the work would've taken him next.

In *Tuesdays With Morrie*, author Mitch Albom quotes his subject, Morris Schwartz, as saying, "Death ends a life, not a relationship." It has felt very natural for me to edit Kevin's poems once more. His voice, as always, was wonderful company. I hope it will be for you, too.

Susan Millar DuMars
January, 2025

I Always Thought I'd Live

Life, Death, & the bit in the middle

Life is books and underwear all over the floor.
Death is everything in its place.
The bit in the middle is mostly waiting for elevators.

Life is a dog barking all night.
Death goes about its business quietly.
The bit in the middle is mostly waiting for the toaster to pop.

Life is a series of clogged sinks.
Death is absolutely clear.
The bit in the middle is mostly hoping
the doctor will call you next.

Life is a philosophy student tossing a sweet wrapper
into your garden, and later
phoning to claim responsibility.
Death is no sweet wrapper ever.
The bit in the middle is mostly thinking
about the phone call you didn't make.

Every life is its own particular mess.
Death arrives impeccably dressed.

Check-Up

As well as blood pressure
the nurse measured my contempt
and told me to stop eating raw steak
while on Twitter. Later,
the x-ray showed my disdain
for the bourgeoisie at levels not seen
since I was fifteen. The optometrist confirmed
my vision is still a little too perfect
for its own good. But the audiologist says
my ears can no longer admit
evidence offered in mitigation for the rich,
idle or otherwise. The bone marrow test
found leucocytes with an unusual hostility
to those who think Oprah Winfrey
might be the answer. My latest liver function result
showed enough bile to make a whole series
of Facebook discussions about politics.
Each of my last twelve colonoscopies
show I'm the sort who holds onto stuff that belongs
down the out-pipe of history.
And the fungus developing under several of my toenails
is the sort that eventually brings down empires;
replaces them with something which, for a time,
has no alternative but to be slightly worse.

To Stability

The consultants agree
your latest bloods and lung function indicate
stability; that you're likely to remain
disastrously alive
as a toothache buzzing like an electric saw
applied to your wide-awake jaw,
alive as a spinal injury
that's an iron claw
shrieking your name
across a white white wall,
alive as a screaming knee
which had to be taken off
in the back of an ambulance
with what felt like a football boot
still stuck in it, alive
as a folksinger made pluck his guitar strings
with fingers smashed in by hammers;

left to come up with some other solution
to the problem of you being you
and this being it.

Mostly

after Victor Meldrew

From there on life is mostly
medicine and cheese;
pills that turn you into an angry fat man.
You dine mostly on soon to be extinct sea slugs.

YouTube videos punctuated
by ads for gambling
and crypto-currency. Gas masks
in the supermarket and no
Garibaldi biscuits anywhere ever.
For the world has run out.

These are the days of muscle spasms
& iron supplements.
Politicians on pretend bicycles
upon whom, your worst days,
you wish cerebral-vascular accidents,
a future of mostly drooling.

Better days you mostly want to pay
someone to steal their saddles
and refuse to give them back
until your demands are met:
Garibaldi biscuits for all.

The Ancestors

The night before my CT scan
they all drop by at once,
throw eyes about the room
which, like myself, is organised
in a disorganised sort of way,
tell me:

I am nothing special
just one in a line
those gone before me
who also lay
alone on mattresses like this
night at the window
offset only by a bare light bulb.

The Man in Room Fourteen

in one crucial respect,
is like everyone else.
He's a working diagnosis
about whom we know
both far too much
and nothing like enough.

The man in room fourteen
spends twenty four hours either
going to the toilet
or not going at all;
is never a happy medium
for happy mediums don't inhabit
rooms like room fourteen.

His wife brings him
a small brown Teddy bear
made (naturally) in China,
which he immediately names
for the Minister For Finance.

The man in room fourteen likely has
somewhere between
two years
and a matter of months.

While other possibilities stalk
elite laboratories
and the walled gardens of certain
medical imaginations;

the man in room fourteen
must now negotiate alone
and from a position of weakness
the narrow track through the dark
that's his only way back away from

the jaws he can hear salivating below him.

Mr Cogito Considers The Side Effects

after Dr. Janusz Krawczyk

Baldness and shortness of breath
a sudden urge to vomit on coats
your own and other people's.
Dry mouth, brittle nails, a tendency
to be not very good at driving
fork-lift trucks and to become even worse
at pole vaulting than you already were.
Explosive watery diarrhea and fecal impaction
sometimes both simultaneously
for the human body likes nothing better
than a good argument with itself.
Infertility, anaemia ,thrombocytopenia,
& Life, Life, Life,
Life itself
are all possible side effects
of drugs such as these.

When I'm Allowed Leave The Cancer Ward

with thanks to Claire Higgins for four of these lines

When I get out of here
I plan to open a factory
that manufactures miniature guillotines
which will be given away gratis
to bullied schoolchildren
to keep hidden in their bedrooms
until I give the signal.

When I get out of here
I plan to finally take that evening class
in Industrial Espionage for Beginners
where I'll learn to break into laboratories
to steal the antidotes
to Elon Musk and
Ursula von der Leyen.

When I get out of here
things will be given their proper names;
the centre of every town re-titled
Oppression Square, during a ceremony
in which the Mayor (or someone prepared
to dress up as the Mayor)
tells the truth about who died,
how, and why.

Worst of all,
I'll start a new Irish Literary Awards
to be held annually at an imaginary hotel.
Categories will include: least authentic
poetry collection, most intellectually empty
novel, most cowardly book review,
publisher who made the biggest
eeijt of themselves this year,
most over obvious networker,
most irrelevant but self-important

anthology, most incestuous
"My Books of The Year" list
in which the author chooses
pals who've all given him
fab reviews too.

And you'll sit there constricting
the exact same muscle
Auntie Mary did when she was in fear
someone was about to take
the Archbishop's name in vain.

On Being Detained At A Medical Facility Four Minutes From Your Own Home

Something is happening in your marrow.
It's D-Day, Gettysburg, Kursk – all of those.
Life is potentially short and savage
but extremely valuable.
Your bloodstream is wild
with uric acid and exploding blast cells.
It is over a fortnight since you went outside.

"This is a very difficult diagnosis."
"These are pills we give to oncology patients."
"Leukemic cells," a young doctor says,
matter of fact, in a bright blue room.
Another doctor, another room,
the word "palliative" is dropped
like a tablet into a glass.
There is a first time for every word
and a last.
And you're not dead yet.

Twenty four hour oxygen.
You realise the song on the soundtrack
on the TV series you're watching
is Highway To Hell
and totally inappropriate,
so turn it up louder.

This soundproof room with windows
that are never unlocked.
You are a few hundred yards from home.
Ginger nut biscuits.

At the window:
the University tower, the Cathedral.
Your everyday familiar
now alien as a postcard

of some German Christmas cake of a town,
abstract as your own front door
and its hallway,
down which you hope to again walk.

This is a difficult diagnosis.
Endstage: pain, delirium, bleeding.
But you're not dead yet,
and can't believe everything
you read on the internet.

There is hope
but you're as afraid of it – almost –
and the lies it might tell you
as you are of its all-consuming absence.

New Reduced Kevin Higgins

I drag myself about the place
like disastrous news
at which people initially
blink their disbelief
until I can drag no more
and have to be fastened
several weeks
to an adjustable white metal bed.

My arse has now mostly vanished
and I must grow a new one.
Certain other key regions
much diminished
lack their usual enthusiasm
and just lie there looking
sorry for themselves.
I can again go to the bathroom
of my own volition
and do so
triumphantly.

Women carry oxygen tanks around for me.
I shuffleplod upstairs
a quarter of a step at a time
then have to slow down for a bit.
I can't see through the freezing fog
to the concluding paragraph of this story.

First time I'm rolled out through the frost
in my gleaming new wheel chair
a whole room tells me
and each other
how great I am
then stand to give me
a round of applause.

It is like attending my own funeral
something I've always wanted to do.

Any News?

It turns out hope is a thing
that expires after thirty days.
Hospital room fourteen
makes way in the mythology
for hospital room nine.

December the twenty third:
the enemy is back
taking ownership of my blood cells
a twenty percent stake so far.

In different words softly delivered
a woman sat on a cushioned purple
mood enhancing chair
tells us this.

Next few days she'll concoct a new plan –
some chemical with a nine or ten syllable name
I can't pronounce –
which we'll call plan C.

On My Death Bed

I will not be calling out to any gods
though I'll probably drop Satan a text to thank him
and his daughters
for some of my more lively afternoons.

I will not be signing forgiveness treaties with the Frauds
but do tell them to stick their heads in the door
when it's least convenient
so I can stare at them and say nothing
and listen to their sphincters creak.

The rest of you who were just being
your honest arsehole selves
I forgive, absolutely
and hope you forgive me
my arseholeness.
There were days
it was all I had to offer.

The Haunting

I don't believe in ghosts
but for you will make an exception
and become one.

When I am all wheezed out
and the tissues, the inhalers
have been put away,
I will start following you everywhere.

You'll think you hear me laughing
in the distance and won't be sure
if it's me still seeing the funny side
of you, or another of your neighbours
putting a sawn-off shotgun in his mouth.

Nights s/he's away and the house
grows creaky with itself,
you'll think you glimpse me
looking in your upstairs window,
or imagine my reflection
in the just deadened TV screen,
or in the water beneath you
each time you try
to go to the toilet.

And when you shudder awake
I'll be stood over you,
my eyebrows grown quite wild,
wearing only a tiny
yellow dicky-bow
which will glare at you like an eye.

The After Life

for Susan

After the sizzle and spit of my flesh going up
like bacon thrown on eight hundred degrees centigrade,
when my bones have been mashed to their final powder,
handed to you in such a civilised pot
and you've flushed
or scattered them – a fistful each –
in the front gardens of those you know hate me
(them that have front gardens; them that don't
put a little of me quietly through their letter boxes) –

I will inhabit the air,
take the form of
the absence of certain smells;
the absence of my tannin caked mug
leaving brown rings behind itself
on the coffee table by the sofa;
the absence of wrong political predictions
I'll no longer be around to deliver
with the wave of an absolute arm
during your favourite TV crime drama,
so you can hear neither
and wish I'd come with a mute button;
the absence of traces of shaving foam
kindly donated by me
in the now pristine bathroom sink
which will gleam at you like the teeth
of a presidential candidate
conceding defeat.

For my absence, like my presence,
will be the mess
you'll never exactly succeed
in completely tidying away.

I Always Thought I'd Live

I always thought I'd live to learn how to swim
do the backward butterfly to Olympic standard
and see trickle-down economics deliver
at least one albeit slightly polluted drop.

I always thought I'd live to learn how to drive,
win at least one Grand Prix motor racing championship
and see the Democrats legislate for free
universal health care.

I always thought I'd live to tidy
the books off the study floor
and see fascists give up
stabbing black boys at bus stops
because peaceful protests
have eloquently made them
see the error of their ways.

But the books that made me
still decorate the study floor
and I don't have the oxygen to shift them.

My consultants are unanimous
my days marching to places like Welling
and Trafalgar Square are over.
The risk of getting tossed into the back of a police van
by over enthusiastic members of the constabulary
is a luxury my lungs can no longer afford.
Even holding a placard in my wheelchair
would soon have me gasping for breath.

And I thought I'd always live.

Waiting For World Peace

This Is Not a Well Made Poem

The well made poem puts on its dicky bow,
walks to the top of the hill,
and has what it calls an epiphany.

The well made poem sees every side of the argument,
except those proscribed by the BBC.

The well made poem has between
twelve and twenty five lines,
all roughly the same length.

The well made poem worries
about Afghanistan (and before that
Vietnam) only when the situation there
might lead to the whole idea
of the well made poem
being vaporised
by a device left at the side of the road.

The well made poem plans to bury
GK Chesterton, William Wordsworth, Sir John Betjeman
and, eventually, Sir Andrew Motion
under its sparkling new patio.

The well made poem never mentions
the puppy processing factory
it knows you own, or your preference
for televised inter-gender wrestling.

The well made poem believes
nuclear weapons are necessary
to keep poems like it safe
from all the rough language
gathered ungovernable at the border
forever threatening to invade.

Congratulations
after Zbigniew Herbert

A few will be obliterated
but in a nice way.
We don't like the word censorship,
abolished it yonks ago.
Certain word combinations must be
nudged to the bottom of the basket
until after we've all safely
choked to death in our dressing gowns.
Though, worryingly,
they always find their way back out again.

Others, we can leave optional.
You know the drift:
the suffering of academics, their divorces
after the regrettable entanglement with the student;
how it felt to phone the crematorium
to book a spot for their ninety five year old father.

But for having so successfully helped it
deny its own existence
the regime has made you
compulsory.

Your personage will be strapped
into an airplane seat, exported
to Asia and beyond,
like a Bangladeshi made t-shirt in reverse.

Your metaphors and similes will be at the service
of the International Happiness Corporation –
Diversity Department –
currently headquartering here for tax purposes.
You will walk through all the right doors
secretly wearing their logo.

Life will be mostly festivals
of enforced grinning,
during which you'll pass the hours
counting each others' teeth.

Facebook Update

after Zbigniew Herbert

I am humbled (and heartfelt) to announce that, in perhaps the greatest honour ever given a poet of my little variety, I've been invited to read my poem 'What Caligula Did Next' at the Emperor's leaving do in the Horti Lamiani Imperial Gardens, Rome next Wednesday. If only my late Mother wasn't ten years incinerated, she'd be so proud. Surely now, National Academy of Burnished Versemakers, here I come! It'd be a red embarrassment for them if I died still outside their walls, yowling like a stray tabby with a toothache, without the official people claiming ownership of me. I can see the scene: insignificant old me being borne through those state-moneyed gold-plated gates on a small throne by six naked minor male poets of advanced years. No one anyone's heard of. Though they've all heard of each other.

Black Notebook, Page 57

after Daniil Kharms

There once lived a curator
with a doctorate in what's
not, whose task
it temporarily was to place
on a high altar
the talking jaws of minor authors
and poets only read by each other
and pay them
to do impressions of themselves.

Nothing in what, for the sake of argument,
we'll call her thoughts
but her own name
bouncing about like a balloon
at a children's birthday party.

Like Chamberlain, Queen Jane,
and Theresa May, she got the job
because of what she wasn't,
and far exceeded
the three person panel's dreams
by being even less than they'd expected.

She was the paragraph
that would've ruined Ulysses,
turned Madame Bovary into a daytime soap opera
that never made it past the pilot,
made Mrs Dalloway cancel the party
and never have people around again;

if it hadn't been surgically excised from the text
by a team from a local creative writing class,
who broke into her apartment
wearing blue plastic gloves
and knew what needed to be done.

Irish Literary Society, 2022

for Rosemary Jenkinson

Wine squeezed into glasses from the corpses
of part-time book reviewers during an autopsy.
A former novelist now reincarnated as a mollusc.
You want to pop him on a cheese-melt
and eat him, though think there's still
a law against that, without his consent
which is unlikely to be forthcoming.
A room full of elderly aunties
terrified someone will actually say something.

Critique

for Alan O'Brien

I hope you won't take this personally
but think your script about a woman starving to death
in a high rise flat which, let's face it, she was lucky to have
in the first place, of limited appeal
to what we'll broadly call people like me.

The scene in which she notices her ribs
poking through her skin
just after the electricity is cut off
and she's unable to call anyone
because her phone is out of credit,
I found oddly lacking in optimism.

One realises such things happen at the margins
and probably more often than is, strictly speaking,
economically necessary. But one must make it relatable
for people who've gone through the Flaubertian trauma
of getting divorced three times in Dalkey
or, worse, not getting divorced at all
in the better portions of Moycullen.

The people I represent demand nuance
in which your script
with its protruding ribs
electricity cut off
and dead mobile is weirdly lacking.

The occasional joke wouldn't go amiss either
particularly at your main character's expense.
It would make her more empathy inducing
for the woman queueing
in the specialist cheese shop,
a key part of our audience.

And a romantic interest,

perhaps with the guy who was her social worker
before the cutbacks–
she keeps mentioning him –
would be a humanising addition.

Otherwise, she's reduced to being a woman who dies
of failing to complete the forms required
to access the relevant supports,
which I'm sure must be out there
somewhere, from some government agency or other.
Or one of those philanthropic trusts who assist such people.

I'm surmising here but find
I generally know what I'm talking about.

Note To Self Re: Evils Of Hipster Careerism In The Literary Arts
after Mel Brooks

What did you expect? "Welcome, sonny"? "Make yourself at home"?
You insist on holding up a flash-lit mirror to their unspeakable parts
again and again (and from every angle)
without giving them a chance to hide
their infections behind a copy
of Tao Lin's latest novel. And yet you're disappointed
the National Nest Egg for The Arts doesn't employ
the daughters (or sons) of the wealthy –
the type who get warm feelings whenever
they hear the word 'poetry' – to fill
your monthly bathtub with salts
enough to make you fizz,
before pampering you all over
until you're supple as newly made
blancmange.

What you've got to remember
is that these are people who think
the Grand Canyon is a metaphor
for the hole inside themselves
they spend forever trying to fill;
that insurrection is wearing
a bowler hat ironically in a restaurant
made of designer Formica and no website.
Folks who, had they been around at the time
would've spent every spare hour liking
the Instagram posts of the late
Leni Riefenstahl. You know,
the sort who went to find themselves
on gap years in Cambodia,
and tragically did.

For All You Know

Nothing is there
in quite the way you see it.
The land your house stands on
is not as you imagine it.
If you listened to what its stones say
you'd know the other side.
The piece of paper that says you own it
is just a thing some guys made up,
like the Book of Deuteronomy
or U.S. constitution.
The woman you're married to
has names of which you know nothing.
The noises coming out of your television set
are not what they claim to be.
Even your doctor is impersonating himself.
The words you have for yourself
are not exactly wrong,
but just a small part of the equation.

Your tactics are something
over which you don't have ultimate control
but a kind of religion
which other people experience
as a series of elbows in the unpleasants
to be repeated
until the next tactic comes along.

The hates you would
if you could
pay someone to wipe way
in a multi-storey car park,
like you just scrubbed
the cat vomit
off the living room carpet.
The woman you want to take to a hotel room
and do things to,

or have her do things to you.
The pair of furrowed eyebrows
(probably false)
who always convinces you,
come election day,
to vote for him.
There is always some secret driving you.

My Permanent Residence

A small apartment in your brain,
from which you'll never evict me
for I throw meat in the mouth
of your screaming need.

At your kind invitation
I take over the grey leather sofa
in your frontal lobe;
sit there flicking through your thoughts,
which time has laminated;
take out your ambitions
and chuckle at their littleness;
listen back to the recordings
things you wanted to say
but didn't think of until I was gone.

I snap the padlock to the granny flat
of your hypothalamus,
change its settings so the taps
are soon gushing pure cortisol
your blood pressure's roaring
and you're seeing apparitions on a screen.

The walls of this place decorated
with hugely unflattering
press clippings
more recent pictures cut from Facebook;
every one of them
me. I star
in the spliced home movie
Your Excuse Filled Life.

Without me
you do not exist.

The Visitor

For so long I wandered the two streets of Headford
with a flashlight,
in the hope of avoiding the likes
of him, for I knew if I was home

to crack open the door when he knocked
the stink of old cheap meat
would pervade any room unlucky enough to have him in it,

that when he's dispatched
via plane, tube, and tragicomic taxi
for a rare winter midweek
to haunt corners he formerly inhabited,
those he meets must afterwards say that,
like hanging will be when it gets brought back,
he's even less fun than they remembered.

For he's the type who spends
the Wednesday evenings of his own perfection
doing things with mince and everybody else's
faults. Most disappointing few seconds of my life,
when I finally met myself.

Brief Reflection On Not Alienating One's Peers

Never say anything which can be misconstrued
or, worse, construed correctly.
If you can avoid it never be either
right or wrong about anything.
When lobbed a direct question
develop what looks like
a kind of facial twitch.

Never suggest they solve their differences
by wrestling naked on the Salthill prom
and never say on social media
you'd be happy to referee such a bout
wearing a three piece suit and a cravat.

Never announce them to the crowd
as Knocknacarra's answer to Norman Mailer
or say on camera that in their absence
"I give you these twelve empty gin bottles".
Keep schtum
when at their book launch or gallery opening
you're handed a plate of cocktail sticks
with nothing at the end of them.

And never arrive at one of their soirees
without having about your person
a magnifying glass through which they appear
as big as they think they are.

Brief Reflection on Hitler

During every argument someone is eventually
Hitler. Both sides of most wars
are now typically Hitler.
History has become a disagreement between Hitler
and a slightly different version of himself.
On the internet
after about the tenth comment
everyone slowly becomes Hitler.
Though hardly anyone has his fashion sense.

In our public squares
there are statues of all sorts of people:
discredited politicians,
generals who won some battle of other,
and saints no one any longer
names their children after,
but hardly any of Hitler.
Except in our heads
where everyone secretly carries
a little statue of Hitler.
God may be gone
but Hitler is everywhere,
which is what he would have wanted.

The Meaning

is the bus that didn't come
the letter you wish hadn't
a car accident no one else survived
a man who now walks with a limp
is a mug one of her students brought her from Cape Cod
an ambulance at five o'clock in the morning
sunflowers bursting up through
a garden that only yesterday
the better quality of dandelion avoided

is realising you went to the wrong funeral
when it's far too late to leave
so you pretend you're someone's uncle
is a solicitor's office complete
with killer mahogany table
a hotel conference room with carpet
that's been used to suffocate people
a meeting that had to be cancelled
another that tragically wasn't

is a man in surgical gloves and a cowboy hat
telling you he's your brother-in-law
is more wine glasses than she could ever have used
two masked men entering a post office
with no intention of robbing it
 a half empty bottle of massage oil
the broken picture frame
they never threw away
a pile of papers that must have meant something

two men on the television
saying slightly different versions of nothing
is a wardrobe that will likely live
to see them carry you out
a phone with messages on it
to be deleted

a framed Soviet propaganda poster
laughing from the living room wall
a wicker chair with nothing on it

but a book of poems
originally written in Polish

For most, is a black car leaving
the street for the last time
For a few, is a body
that was never identified.

Downstairs

after Charles Simic

They reassure themselves with the voices:
Sir David Attenborough and Morgan Freeman.
They do not know their children are upstairs
putting Barbie and Ken on toy guillotines;
their little plastic necks no match
for what's hurtling their way.
Afterwards, the cat, now Chief Prosecutor
for the new reconstituted
Committee for Public Safety
chases their heads around the room
and retrospectively finds
every one of them guilty.

Ballad of The Crank

Today the crank has a Dublin accent
that's like someone's head being opened with a chisel
on Jervis Street after the last DART has failed to materialise.
Tomorrow the crank will turn up talking
a new improved superior class of accent altogether.

The crank used to want to go and live in South Africa
but since they ruined it
has transferred his affections to Israel.
Whenever he thinks of Belfast before the Troubles
the crank gets nostalgic
squeezes some tears into the tiniest bottle in history
and sends them to the Sunday Independent letters section.

Every time there's a new Minister for Justice
the crank writes to them
outlining the real world necessity
of a certain amount of police brutality.
When they legalised abortion
the crank began saying the Rosary twice a night.
Before that, he used to go to discotheques
dressed as Richard Dawkins.

The crank sits beside you at a poetry reading
and afterwards tells you
how killing Chilean folksingers
and plopping their mashed bodies on the street
is sometimes for the greater good.
The crank spends a lot of time thinking
about men in dresses
and picturing what they do with
what's underneath their dresses.

When the authorities finally catch up with you
the crank types "at last"
over a picture of you being carried

into the back of the big black van.
The crank has a secret picture book:
The Uniforms of Policemen Down the Ages
thinks the world would be better
if everyone went around the place
dressed as their own private police man.

A Life Disappointed

By the savagery of the light
the bloodiness of your arrival
and the sound of your own name
By the shape of the seat
before ever you sat in it
By the bacon, the sausages,
and the plate they came on
By the songs the band sang
and by those they forgot
By the extent of your losses
in the magnifying glass
and the littleness of your victories
in the blinder of your eyes
By other people's cats
and the trucks that eventually
run them all over

First by there and now by here
Almost as much by up
as you were by down
Even more by in
than you were by out
By the temperature of the crematorium
the claustrophobia of the box

According To Our Intelligence Reports

Yours is a life defined
by an admirable absence of hyperbole.
Up, for you, never nears
any potentially calamitous mountain tops
down never even thinks of rummaging
in the Queen of the Underworld's panties and bra.

The curries you concoct
for your legendary Friday evening knees ups,
which always end early and without incident,
are the mildest kormas this side
of the calmer parts of Bedfordshire.

You pleasure yourself slightly less
than the average male of your age and species
and always without unseemliness
or endangering the supply line
of Kleenex during times of contagion, war,
and generalised roaring at the television.

When you reach your expiration date
you won't be buried or burnt
or fritter public money dribbling
in some sad facility on the outskirts
but without comment or proclamation
be politely tidied away.

The Secret Life

The places he goes
when his wife thinks he's at the pharmacy.
The conversations she loves
not having with him
while he's wherever that is.
The pictures he keeps in a folder
titled 'people who've forgotten my name'.
The things he put in a suitcase
he thinks is still in the attic;
home to generations of mice
which he hopes have eaten the evidence.
The lies he keeps in his phone.
The women he keeps in his basement,
though they've all long since gnawed
through the bonds of their poor choices
and married other people.
The pictures he keeps on a computer
he can only access in the locked room
he sneaks off to bank holiday weekends
to set up Facebook accounts in the names
of women who don't exist
to send messages to his designated enemy
and, when the time comes,
his enemy's widow.

Apartment 5E

after Rod McKuen

The old woman upstairs is again engaging
in multi-partner Sadomasochism.
I set my watch
by the yelps and screams wafting
through my ceiling.

I see her often abseiling
down the side of the building
in her bloodstained overcoat,
or shuffling off at night
to the used leather goods shop.

Every Hanukah early morning
I hear her playing heavy metal
music at top volume,
or stomping overhead
in her replica World War Two
German Army boots.

For Christmas,
she brings me letters she says
the postman misdelivered –
hospital appointments,
final reminders, and, once, a death threat –
all of them addressed to The Occupier.

Things He Isn't Paid To Remember

That his job as an educator
is to make people's minds
more blank than they already are
That to bow before the trinity
of painted fruit bowls, new kitchens, and lyric poetry
could put one on the wrong side of pretty much everything,
history included
That a European army might not be the answer we're looking for
That even the no his herringbone wool jacket
doesn't want to absorb
is still no
and there's no use blaming the lighting
or the Russians on those occasions
when the one thing the situation doesn't require
is more people like him
That there are scumbags out there
who make it their business to notice
the things about which he says nothing
That his powers of persuasion are there to keep the doors shut
on certain rooms with strange smells in them
to help make sure once again
the good guys win in the end.

To The Man Who Lost His Shadow

Though experts believe you still exist in theory
have lately visited certain hospitals
and, last week, a post office;
many of the younger generation think
you're a story the old people made up
to scare them.

Your immediate family meet annually
to celebrate having forgotten you entirely.

You still plod some street or other
one that's been scrubbed from the map
but even your shadow has abandoned you.

Those who spent years arguing
there was no alternative to you
needed someone
worse than themselves to reassure them
when they glimpsed their own reflections
in the ravenous river's gleam.

I Will Survive

after Gloria Gaynor

Though you didn't ask,
have to say, I'm proud
as a giant ginger cat
with the sofa to itself
that while my co-conspirators
were being led into the back
of police vans having been
caught in possession of the wrong
haircut for the new weather,
I never once fell into the trap –
as all the others did –
of being unnecessarily rude
to my interrogators. Quietly grew
my hair to meet the new
legal requirements
while everyone else
was self indulgently
never heard of again.

Furthermore, I made it through
the authorities smathering my friends –
one after another – in baby oil
and releasing them into
the Belgian Congo to fend
(or not) for themselves
without once stooping
to sarcasm or expletives
as almost anyone else
in my position would have.

I survived the Moscow Trials,
all belonging to me being convicted
of terrorism, espionage, and meeting
the German Ambassador in a non-existent hotel,
without once losing my temper.

Because politeness never killed anyone,
with the possible exception
of him, and her, and them.

And I plan to deliver myself
safely to the mortuary
without once having cried,
except for my secret, sobbing self.

Sketch of Mr & Ms Past Tense

after Wallace Stevens

They're in one of the smaller mansions on the shore
that isn't holding up against the hurricane
but refuse to leave because nothing is happening
and this is at most a blip.

Where they are there will soon be no there.
But his principles and her standards
are overreach become shortfall.

The humanoids in their basement,
attic, boiler house are free to leave
anytime they find somewhere better to be.

Those that remain scratch their complaints
on the un-papered walls
for they know no better;

nor care that when you're past tense
there is nothing else
but the hurricane and all it makes
mere debris to be tossed out of tomorrow's way.

Common Sense Climbed Out of the TV the Other Night

And sat beside me on the settee,
its shirt white, its manner mild
as an unsugared cornflake.

Confident as a New York Times Op-Ed
written by God.

Thought provoking in conversation
as a dinner party at which
the main course always tastes
suspiciously like Melvyn Bragg.

I could see from its resumé
it was well thought of by those that matter
like a Hampstead charity shop
in which Joan Bakewell
is now available free of charge.

Though it kept trying
to avoid catching my eye,
when it did, the shiver I got
told me it would be supportive,
when the going got hot,
as a crutch made of butter.

Later, it climbed into my computer
where its tweets against the turning world
looked like they'd been typed in the day room
of a care home for former provosts
of Queen's College Oxford.

It expressed itself with such authority
I had to test its advice by taking it.
And it turned out to be as sensible
as running through a forest fire
in a grass skirt.

Your Days of Total Disdain

Polite society was a cat that paid tribute
to you by ignoring you completely.
The daylight greeted you as a sex worker would
a client with a taste for the peculiar.
Your evenings were a secret club
with a washing line strung
across an impromptu dance floor.
Back when you were so thin
you'd slip under their door like a leaflet
for dry cleaning or getting their gutters done –

though afterwards they'd deny you,
as if they'd all had their eyes picked out
by some mollusc eating
whiskey drinking giant with a tweezers.

And you'd go off about your business
like a toad proud of its warts.

Anxiety Prayer

Oh Miseria, help me accept the things
I could have changed, but rage
against stuff which was always
going to turn out that way anyway.

May I always leave the front door
unlocked but dash shrieking
up into the attic whenever
anyone opens it.

May I never remember to put on
a swim suit before getting into
a hot-tub with a sexually overwrought
former Governor of Arkansas.

May I not use the eye drops as prescribed
until shortly before my better left eye
has to be scooped out with an emergency spoon,
leaving me to roam my little bit of the Earth
looking like Long John Silver's sister.

May I get taken to court
for inadvertently chopping down
my next door neighbour's tree,
and defuse the situation by head
butting the judge.

May I drown out the tragic music
of local boneheads trying out their new
meat cleaver on the Latvians across
the road with my sobs about what
Ferdinand and Isabella did to the Jews.

May I never wear protective clothing
when entering a burning nuclear power plant
or a dysfunctional woman from Dundalk.

Take from me the wisdom
to ever know the difference.

Burden Sharing

after Jonathan Swift

Your threadbare cat, Eric,
who never came back –
and the two puppies you recently found throttled –
are a laugh a nanosecond compared
to my sad hamster still loitering tragically
in the corner of his cage.

Your sprained ankle
though impressively black
and blue, stands not a chance
against my suspected skin cancer
which I plan to let mature
a while.

Your root canal surgery
later this afternoon is no match
for what I think is
rigor mortis
in my left elbow.

The fact that your entire family
died in that car crash
half an hour ago –
and you probably won't
recognise them in the mortuary –
is nothing compared to how I feel
since I realised people
are, for some reason,
starting to avoid me.

And the head injury you'll get
when you fall down the stairs
after talking once more to me
is small when set against
the surprising over-reaction

of the alligator I yesterday poked
with a too short stick.
You would not believe
how it altered its personality for the worse.
When you're back on your feet,
or even when you're not,
I'll come tell you all about it.

Potential

The ball in the air,
soaring as it must between
fantastic and catastrophe.
The world looks at you and gasps.

You could end up having
medals pinned on you
by the King of Sweden
or dine out for life on the thinnest
anecdote in history:
that cup final penalty
you send so wide
they still haven't found the ball.
Or, if you're that special type of unlucky,
both. And have to sell the medals
to a guy born
with that sheep-skin jacket
already attached.

The trajectory not yet certain
as in those movies
in which one of the bad guys
always wears a white suit.

That you'll finish up a failed alcoholic
unable any longer to drink
who just sits there being
an angry type of sad,
is not yet written.

The Joke

after Walter Benjamin

A barrel of industrial waste poured into a suit
donated by a casino owner who knows people
with a tangerine tea towel tossed strategically on top
because it was the only available metaphor for hair
was running for re-election as CEO of South Canadia
against an old coat with holes in it.

The barrel of waste was trailing
histrionically among professors emeritus
whose brains were in the process of being dismantled
by lethargy and time, and among those
who, as and when the stock market permits,
take a year off to celebrate their dividends
by doing good works among brown people in far countries
not lucky enough to have stock markets or dehumidifiers.
Such people agreed with each other that the barrel of waste
made the raging boil on the nation's privates
way too obvious, and hoped by throwing
the old coat over it they could again
forget it was there.

The barrel of waste said the old coat couldn't deliver
on the promises he wasn't making,
and maintained good leads among morticians,
pimps, and police informants
and had the total bastard vote
ninety nine percent sewn up –
in essence everyone except the late John DeLorean
and perhaps Alan Dershowitz.

There was a minority faction who wanted the boil
on the nation's privates given free antibiotics, lanced
with a big needle imported from Sweden
and then cauterised. But most people found
though they were in favour, in their hearts,

of lancing the boil,
in practice they were for
allowing the boil to grow redder, angrier, more toxic
under the old coat with holes in it.

So the minority extremist faction
who wanted the thing treated
were sentenced to the echo chamber
to argue about whether the old coat
with holes in it really
was the lesser evil.

The midwife of history,
grown bored with the year twenty twenty,
had decided to play one of her jokes.

The Biden Monologues: Day 457

America as a notion can be defined as a single word.
Most days that word is:
        meatloaf
        gasoline
        hamburgers
        Cher
        or Batman
others days it's
        cowgirl
        sunglasses
        alligator
        spandex
        motel
though those allegations are unproven.
America is a saxophone
that denies everything;
    a banjo
with two torn strings;
    a Cadillac
with a black woman
who may have been part Cherokee
in its trunk. At least we think
it was a woman. Police
assure me
they're looking into it.
    And when we kid ourselves
the children aren't listening
the word is:
        washroom
        billionaire
        sniff
        transvestite
        Israel
excuse me, I mean
        wigwam
        railroad

       Mexico
       nothing
these are national security matters
covered by the relevant legislative get-out clauses
and just alligators at this stage.
I was in the foothills of the Rockies
       the Catskills
       the Alps
       the MaGillycuddy Reeks
chewing over the world conundrum with
       Joshua Nkomo
       King Zog
       Micheál Martin
       or was it
       Liberace?
I can't be sure any of this is true.

To My Friends Who Said Nothing During the Witch-hunting of Ilhan Omar

Those who stuck to the practical stuff,
people-carrying your children – all
of whom are now at least seven foot tall –
to soccer or lacrosse,
or to paraphrase Malcolm X at the intervarsity
debating championship;

sympathised with yourself
by buying for yourself tickets
to see Jackson Browne sing songs –
three consecutive nights –
about what's really going on.

Your political integrity, the apple
that went off in the bowl
all that time no one was looking, collapsed
rotten in the hand of the first person
who picked it up and tried
to take a clean, clarifying bite.

Now you prove your maturity
and commitment to demawcracy
by secretly buying Israeli oranges
and daring yourself to eat them.

Utopia American Moderates Dreamt Into Being

Executions, if they continue, as they must,
for public opinion demands them, and who
are you to disagree with people like you,
will be carried out in a timely and efficient manner:
injections of genetically modified wasp venom
to the heart, eye, or groin
rather than people's heads going on fire in the chair.
The investment community can rest reassured
the procedure will be exclusively reserved
for those who grew up chasing each other
across the nearest available communal concrete.

And we'll spend the money previously squandered
allowing welfare queens to push out
future liabilities, without due
consideration for people like you,
on razor wire we'll contract
the now, thankfully, more racially diverse
American Chamber of Commerce
to decorate the concrete perimeters
of penitentiaries where boys from the projects
will go to repent the crime of having
employed bad lawyers, and learn
to contribute to the economy
as every citizen will,
if they know what's good
for them. I mean: us.

In the long run, they'll thank us,
for such people have a deep
appreciation of concrete;
it brings back pictures
of their happy childhoods
which were, for the most part,
all about the concrete.

I Am an American Leftist

Since I got to Congress I say: #MedicareForAll
with the seagull stare of someone – gender unspecified –
supple enough to have relations with Governor Gavin Newsom
while wearing an Even My Dog Hates Gavin Newsom t-shirt

In my youth I used to quip: ballistic missiles
should be funded by charity auctions
attended by retired golf professionals
and eminent colorectal surgeons.

I used to, generally speaking, be against nuclear annihilation
until Donald Trump said something about Russia.
Now, it's what the blue side wants. And who am I to go playing
Rosa Luxembourg when there's proper politics to be done.

I believe in the one true NATO and the FBI.
I'm all about the big initials.
Instead of taking the soft option of abolishing it,
I now want to put the 'I' back into the CIA

These days, each time I vote "present"
on the defence budget, I Spotify
the theme tune from Flash Gordon
and marvel at my maturity.

Fetish in Which I Visit The Early 1950s (USA style)

I go about the place dressed as a rich liberal
with homes on both coasts.

I attend philanthropic evenings
alongside tennis players you've never heard of
and psychiatrists yet to be discredited.

Above my mantelpiece hangs
a framed black and white photograph
of a man wearing a pince-nez.
I tell people he was my great grandfather.

I cry the day the Rosenbergs are tied
to the chair and set on fire,
but understand why it has to be this way.

I allow myself some celebratory French toast
the morning the Times tells me
our boys have retaken Seoul.

I am in favour of giving civil rights to the negro, eventually
but don't get carried away.
For the world is kept together by people like me
not getting carried away.

I believe in world peace and invest in Dow Incorporated.

I understand why President Truman had to authorise
'Little Boy' and 'Fat Man'
but feel sorry for the dreams it must give him.

The Death By Drowning Of Twenty Seven Migrants In The English Channel on Wednesday
November, 2021

It could have been twenty seven Cliff Richard fans
who quite like that Boris Johnson really;
twenty seven Noel Edmonds lookalikes
whose wives stimulate themselves with The Daily Express;
twenty seven former double glazing salesmen from Folkestone, Kent
who blame everything on the French;
twenty seven members of the Murdoch extended family
(including Jerry Hall);
twenty seven known business associates of the Duke of York;
twenty seven potential Archbishops of Canterbury;
twenty seven people with Allegra Stratton accents;
twenty seven arthritic comedians who spent
four years making Diane Abbott quips;
twenty seven recovering logical positivists
who get their political philosophy from the tweets
of Right Said Fred, Joanna Lumley, & David Baddiel;
twenty seven OBEs, MBEs, and Commanders of The British Empire.

But, tragically, it wasn't.

How To Survive Next Winter

Turn off the heat.
Instead, warm yourself by setting fire
to your free weekly copy of The Galway Advertiser.
Be sure and arm yourself with extra
by liberating them from your neighbours' letter boxes.
Sit in the dark, preferably alone,
so you don't spread the pox to anyone else,
wearing a cheap pair
of unsustainable sunglasses;
they're the only luxury we'll allow you.
Get extra underwear second hand
from your local mortuary;
I hear they plan to start selling them
out of the back of the hearses
for which they can no longer afford petrol.
There are bargains to be got.
Exercise personal responsibility.
Begin eating spiders, dandelions
and – for calcium – each other's toenails.
But only as a weekend treat.
The notion of eating each day
is a pre-war social construct.
Spend the October bank holiday
rolled up in an old carpet,
and Christmas writing Limericks:
there was a young man from Killiney
whose plans for world domination were stymied...

The Abolition of What's Next

It is ten to whenever
and must remain so.

The living room door
will remain ajar
at exactly that angle.

The cat will forever
have just opened its eyes
having heard something worrying.

Your dinner will remain unprocessed
in the various departments of your gut.

You will never have sex
or go the toilet again.

What is coming,
though it will never get here,
is January, February, and Death.

30-12-20

The Angry

No group angers me more
than the angry.
If only they'd cool it, they'd see as I do
life is actually pretty okay.
No one murders them in their beds (yet).
They almost always
have to get up, go outside,
walk around a bit, maybe light a cigarette
or try to buy a bar of chocolate
before the police kill them.

Their inability to tell us in exact words
what the fuck they want
has me punching the TV screen
at their inarticulacy.
Coming across all unreasonable
never got anyone
the kind of private health insurance
that fixed, in good time,
my deviated septum
and my fist when I broke it
against our marble kitchen countertop
while making a perfectly valid point
about people like them.

They can't expect people like me to swallow
the dry bread of their slogans
flavoured only with the salt of their curses.
Some of which I had to look up on the internet
to make my disdain so complete I snapped
my new blue mid-life-crisis glasses
in two, must now buy another pair
and they likely won't be available
in quite the same blue,
which just makes me fume.

Deliberately Offensive Song

> *"A street performer shall not act, say, do or sing anything likely to cause alarm, distress or offence to any member of the public, business owner, the Council, or any member of An Garda Síochána."*
>
> Galway City Council bylaw as of 2-1-2020

Despite the Alderman, his head a sweaty pink moon,
who wanted travellers castrated,
or at least kept behind an electric fence.

Despite the former Mayor who liked to taste
the thighs of teenage boys in a local pub's
musty meeting room and wore
his ceremonial robes while doing it.

Despite the motion you passed overwhelmingly
against contraceptive devices and students
engaging in sensuality without responsibility.

Despite the fortune one of your number got
from coffin ships his grandfather
profitably fed to the starving
Atlantic sharks.

Despite the "dastardly" Rising
at whose failure you rejoiced and the diamond
welcome you gave Edward the Seventh.

Despite the lines of white powder expertly
inhaled off a professional lady's
clavicle which none of your number
knew anything about.

You are inoffensive as a fairground
run by defrocked priests in grey raincoats;

inoffensive
as a former Mayor owning
a seafront casino that took
the pensions of passing widows,
the disability benefits
of bald guys with the shakes;

inofuckingffensive
as a line of giant white puddings
who've calamitously been
let talk.

The Dialectics of Irish

after Francois Villon

There is no great starvation
without someone somewhere keeping the trout paté for later,
no t-bone steak at The Shelbourne (rare or well done)
without bales of straw being dragged through January mornings,
no plate of cabbage without the possibility
of an open safety pin camouflaged within it like a terrorist,
no refusal of a cup of tea
that's not a potential resumption of hostilities,
no glass of high end whiskey
you can be sure the night porter
didn't celebrate his departure
by lacing with high end Dublin piss –
though these days he's mostly from Latvia or Killybegs –
no problem that can't be made worse
by a pair of fashionable glasses whose big idea
is a poetry competition sponsored by Guinness
on the theme of black and white.

There is no *Tá* without *Níl*,
no *no* without the wink of other possibilities,
no card game that can't finish up with everybody losing,
no peace talks to which the dead aren't invited,
no ballot box in Leitrim without the ghost of an ArmaLite,
or the actual metal of a Heckler & Koch
Garda submachine gun in the hands of
a large farmer's son from County Meath,
no pint of Guinness that can't be made worse
by a poem about peace
shouted out by a pair of fashionable glasses.

There's no wealth like empty office blocks,
no talent like the country's least favourite novelist,
no generosity like an Anglo-Irishman taking
his ten gallon hat out for the evening,
no wisdom like a Leinster rugby fan

screeching for war with Russia,
no courage like informing,
no place in the minds of the nation's keenest intellects
that exists less than Creggan, Ballymurphy, Crossmaglen...
and no poem about all this
that can't be made more unpalatable
by a pair of fashionable glasses
trying to sell you the best of all possible
pints of what might be Guinness.

Redefining Ireland

"Ireland must reassess military power"
SIMON COVENEY

In the absence of Seamus Heaney,
if Ireland is to be renowned for anything other
than bog water, cabbage and
our negligible corporate tax rate,
we must invest in at least one
intercontinental ballistic missile
which until the necessary
Plutonium – 239 gets here
we'll fill with hydrogen sulphide
reinforced regularly
courtesy of our world famous piggeries
and drag it to every St. Patrick's Day parade
from Castlerea to Bantry
because people need something to celebrate.

Instead of the perfect simile
we'll offer annihilation
for somewhere roughly the size of Iceland.
Instead of metaphors we'll give you death
immediate or lingering
(terms and conditions will be applied
no liability admitted).
Instead of the occasional Haiku
we'll build a leprechaun Little Boy
put it in a box
then skulk the Earth
looking for someone to drop it on.

She had, she thought, a thousand things to say

after Edmond Jabé

Of the Trinity school of journalese
she was a product.
And when they were told to
people bought her;
put her on their marble finish kitchen counters
and dreamed of world war three and four
and liked her monotone clack so much
they plopped another two Euro coin in the relevant slot
so they could hear once more
everyone she disagreed with
or whose fabulous hair she was jealous of
be called Chinese spies.

And all the other little journalesers
rushed in to squeak their weasel agreement
apart from the predictable elements
who were, naturally, just more Chinese spies.
As people like her tend to
she got what she wanted
lots of people saying her name
though not all of them pronounced it right
and some of them were barely people.
And, eventually, both world wars
                three
                      and four.

And there were no more marble kitchen tops.
No more two Euro coins.
Nor slots to plop them in.
And, from her, no more squeaks.
Best of all there were no more four wheel drives
or children to drive to sporting events in them.
We all died happily ever after
apart from the Chinese spies and their acolytes
who died most unhappily.
But there's no pleasing some people.

And Now For The Future

from the original Gaelic

Epsom Derby winner Shergar
missing almost forty years
will be found – clip clop –
in the townland of Stuck.
Will from now on have a column in
the Irish Mail On Sunday
in which he will express
increasingly right wing views.

After its next war
America will be no longer there
to play *mine's
biglier than yours* with China.
The territory which previously
traded under that name
will be governed by friendly
Eritrean troops whose long term task
will be to teach its people to survive
without ordering knick knacks from catalogues.

Satan, or as we in the Future Room call her,
the leader of Her Majesty's opposition,
will buzz off to another galaxy
because her work here is done;
dining as she goes on a sponge cake
made from the testicles of Russian oligarchs
and Clinton campaign operatives.

University education will be phased out
as there'll be nothing worth knowing,
the campuses used as care homes
for insane ex-politicians
who'll wander mostly without clothes,
being their leathery selves,
muttering in the local language
"I'm glad you asked me that question."

Silicon Valley will be placed
behind suitably toothy barbed wire,
repurposed as a detention archipelago
for former internet trolls
sentenced to have Mark Zuckerburg masks sewn
onto their faces.

The philosopher A.C. Grayling
and the bones of Isaiah Berlin
will be sold to the Tunisians.

The remaining Earthlings
will mostly huddle in the dark
playing remember when,
until one day nobody does.

And a child picks up
a decommissioned smart phone,
and asks what it is.

The entire staff, except the cleaners,
of both the Brookings
and American Enterprise institutes
will be granted
their own personal nuclear submarine,
from where they'll continue
to try to rule us.

The weather forecast will be discontinued
as there will be no way of telling
what's coming from where.
Some will revert to offering prayers
to traditional and refurbished gods.
During hurricanes a few will gather
at what they believe
is Tom Cruise's grave
and ask him to intervene.

And Ryanair will start offering to instead take you
to the middle of nowhere by rowing-boat.

August 15th, 2021

The day the Taliban retook Afghanistan
I went out into the garden
and killed the last few butterflies.

The day the Taliban retook Afghanistan
I refused to recycle anything.

The day the Taliban retook Afghanistan
I got the whole family, including the cat,
to take up smoking.

The day the Taliban retook Afghanistan
I ate an entire packet of hydroxychloroquine
in the hope I might get blistering, or peeling skin,
around the mouth, lips, and genitals.
But was sadly disappointed.

The day the Taliban retook Afghanistan
I watched Carry On Up The Khyber
over and over again.

The day the Taliban retook Afghanistan
I sat at my desk and squiggled an order
that those who have been this wrong
never again speak.

But their jaws still creak open.
And sounds come out.

It All Depends

It depends what the meaning of "is" is,
which depends what the meaning of "isn't" is,
which depends what you mean by "my hand",
which depends what I mean by not "around her waist".

It depends on the meaning of "know",
which depends on the meaning of "don't",
which depends on the meaning of
    "a house in Belgravia",
which depends on the meaning of
    "March the tenth",
which depends on the meaning of
    a "Pizza Express in Woking".

It may also depend what the meaning of
    "Prince Michael of Yugoslavia" is,
what the meaning of "Annabel", "Maxine", and "Amber" is,
what the meaning of "Jeffrey's apartment for models" is,
what the meaning of Brian Ferry's phone number is,
what the meaning of "people from the United Nations" is,
and what the precise meaning of "going on" is,
which may well depend, for all I know,
on what the meaning of "Linda Spankman masseur" is.

It definitely depends what is meant by "foot massage",
which depends on what you mean by "down",
what I mean by "there",
and what we both understand
by "young Russian woman".

And it all turns on the significance we attach
to the words: "nothing", "happened",
and "at most three times".

Cometh the hour, cometh the Dame

after John Cooper Clarke

the fucking dame is fucking furious
and not fucking having it
fucking up is fucking down
fucking in is fucking out
fucking master is fucking slave
fucking Palestine is fucking never
fucking Goliath is fucking David
fucking catapult is fucking atom bomb
the fucking wall was fucking built
to keep the fucking Arabs off
the fucking land fucking snatched
fucking fair and fucking square

and if you lot dare
say I stalk about the fucking
House of Commons spitting
words like 'fucking' or mention
the fucking bust of fucking Lenin
I fucking bought and fucking placed
in Islington Town fucking Hall when
I was first elected fucking queen
you'll be hearing from
the fucking lawyer my fucking hubby
gifted me our first night together
sincerely fucking yours, Margaret Hodge

Hell's Most Boring Room

Its door creaks ajar to reveal:

your least favourite aunt's Pekingese
trying to chew an original copy of The Treaty of Maastricht
though for lack of teeth
failing.

Everyone who ever asked John Major for his autograph,
except those who wanted it on an intimate body part.

The guy who on every key vote
abstained.

Just to be on the safe side,
all daytime TV presenters ever
with the honourable exemption of those using it
as a come down gig from a cocaine addiction.

The guy who phoned the government to tell them
what you get up to at weekends.

The woman who thinks the worst thing in the world
is plumbers who don't pay all their taxes;
for it is written that she will be provided
with an appropriate parking space in Hell
for her bicycle.

The guy who got elected
chair of his residents' association by accident;
he thought he was going to the chiropodist
but went in the wrong door
and was too disgustingly polite to leave.

The Europe correspondents of every newspaper
and TV Station on Earth.

And above all the people
who due to lack of imagination
charged too low a price
for selling out their friends.

White

for Suad Aldara

Now they are bombing white people!
With bombs not officially signed off on
by the people who sign off on such things.

Television and internet are laden
with white people fleeing their houses
many of which are no longer technically houses
into any country that'll have them
which is pretty much any country they want.

The leader of the white people
flashes around the world,
or at least your smart phone,
dressed as a hero.

Elderly white women everywhere
pray he'll marry their daughters;
a few, even, that he'll take one
of their bachelor sons as his wife.

White people everywhere race
to register their sorrow for those
whose white bones and even whiter faces
make them ill suited to having
bombs dropped on them.

Those of us who live in half a shed
will happily share our half a shed with
the white people; their children, if needs be,
can rest their heads on our mousetraps

and we'll all be heroes,
which is well and good
but when will the world get back to
just bombing brown people?

Temple of Electricity

after Enrique Linh

Your wages are mine
and so, if I want it, is your father's life
and your little son's
little life and your daughter's
but I let you go free
as long as you say
anything
apart from having done that
and seen it twist out this way
we won't be doing it again.

Because we will.
I have already ironed
our light grey uniforms.

What we do
will gain its electricity
from us knowing how
it turns out.

This time can take bets
on where the blood spatters
might land.

Safe To Say

How ghastly the day before yesterday was
now everyone associated with it is dead.
In the future I'll be against
what's going on now.
I'll be on the television,
horrified. But not yet.

As a civilised person,
I'm absolutely in favour of the nice policeman now,
one hundred percent against the tear gas and dogs
you forced him to use on you back then.

Sometime the century after next
I'll be against giving the children of Bethlehem
something from Lockheed Martin
to occupy themselves with for Christmas.
Like I was against rhino-whipping the blacks
into line in Port Elizabeth, Ladysmith, Pietermaritzburg
after it stopped happening.
But, for now, see no alternative.

22/12/2021

After The Defeat

People who never did anything in the first place
talk about giving up; text you
from the ruins of their overworked armchairs,
while you're stuck breathing in diesel
and death on the beach at Dunkirk.

TV studios crowd with
suddenly undead experts, all come to tell you,
now we know the chemotherapy
hasn't worked as you'd hoped,
it's time you took up smoking again
to see if that helps.

Devils prowl internet and Earth,
dressed in clothes almost identical to yours,
and whisper in voices
part Siren picking her lyre, part bark of jackal,
part your worst self whining,
that the only way you'll be rid
of war, Jacob Rees Mogg, and poor people
dying of being poor

is if you desist from further silliness
and click the box to sign up
to their generous introductory offer

of a little more war, Jacob Rees Mogg
and poor people dying because they deserve it.
Terms and conditions to follow.

The Old Accusation

It always comes back, like the crows.
One of them parks himself at your elbow,
ironed into his golfing jumper
or the jacket his late mother bought him
to celebrate his divorce.

He squawks in your face
– *only jokin' like* –
the hint of the garlic mushrooms
that were, in the end, a disappointment:
that it was people like you,
your head polluted with Lenin, Leon,
that mad German economist,
and a million wriggling excuses
in every possible language.
It was people like you
who shot the Czar and his family.

You try to smile.
He growls slightly:
*you think it funny
to kill children for politics.*
You might as well
have pulled one of the triggers yourself,
driven your bayonet into that sick child's chest.
It was people like you
who afterwards washed
the brain off the wallpaper,
cut the jewels from their clothes.
It was people like you.

Glancing at the rain
flecking the hotel bar window, you tell him:

from the look of the wet cardboard
shanty town growing piecemeal,
like a fungus,
in the night time doorways of this city,
it'll soon be time we went back down there
and killed them again.

Exercise In Democracy

We as a society are suffering from a malaise.
Our leaders no longer live in sufficient terror
of being chopped to bits like red peppers
in their own boudoirs,
or the boudoir of their least favourite mistress,
cocker spaniel, tarantula, swimming coach, or dentist
(each to their own) by an axe
attached to a man or woman
with certain criticisms of government policy.
Or at least the manner in which aspects
of government policy are being implemented.

Any damage done to tarantulas,
least favourite mistresses, or cocker spaniels
during this process will be entirely incidental.
The upside: the boost to the economy
of the exponential increase in the sale of axes.
Soon every town will have a factory
manufacturing them, many with the words
we as a society
carved into their handles.

1996

Storms have, the experts concur,
been abolished. There will soon
be no further need for forecasts.

There are still occasional rumours:
weather events in places of no concern
to men in patterned sweaters
or the women who stick
said sweaters in the washer-dryer for them.

But no dark voices in the radio.
No old oaks or sycamores
come crashing anywhere near here.
Our dramas microscopic;
the little unWagnerian soap operas
of it being 1996.

I rent an upstairs room,
fill it with cheap despair,
poetry and the sound of
what might be the smallest
of orgasms, its teeth clenched
or a hand over its mouth.

When asked my occupation
I type: retired philosopher
on my first ever elderly desktop computer.
I don't tell the nice woman from the government.
But, from the cruit on me,
she knows. And is okay with it.

We believe the story
of next year
and the year after won't be only
virus, invasion,
and maybe sitting in the dark.

Sunday September the 24th, 7.10pm

I have finally tracked you down.
Or at least am in the same city as you now.
I see from social media you
arrived a couple of days ago and are
looking for any excuse to give yourself
another round of applause.
You are telling them the story
about how, as a boy, your family once
had their telephone cut off.
But that won't be happening again.

From the maturity of your response
to the absurd pleading
of those who hoped
to be let out of the basement
and given some air,
it's crystal
there'll be none of that nonsense
on your watch
but free flags for everyone
which must at all times be carried
or flown by anyone who doesn't want
their passport suspended.

For the exchequer-funded undead
who skuttle about the kingdom in medieval dress
the festival will continue.
Basement dwellers
will be allowed out appointed days
to watch their betters go past
and wave their happy little flags.

The twilight coming down on me,
as I wait for the airport taxi that will carry me
closer again to you,
is the same twilight you'd see

if you ever did anything so average
as look out a window.
Too busy kangarooing room to room
being extravagantly pleased with yourself.

In private, your anger is a big fish
thrashing on the deck of a trawler
desperate for somewhere to go
which is why, according to my sources
you sometimes throw
office furniture around the place.

You don't know me
yet. But I know what time
you'll be at the restaurant,
made my reservation this morning.
I'm enjoying
the thought of your face

Waiting for World Peace

after Muriel Rukeyser

She says she'll be with me any moment,
and we'll run naked through meadows together.
Right now she's busy consulting her diplomats,
a bunch of guys with white hair
who know nothing of war
but lots about maps and how to redraw them.
Any moment now, she'll get
to be entirely herself.
First she must address the Security Council,
dressed as the ghost of Madeleine Albright.
Then get around the heaviest table in history
with people whose companies
do their bit for peace
by developing more efficient
weapons systems
and making war unthinkable.

Any second now,
once she's invaded
the few remaining places considered a threat
to us running naked through meadows together.
Nowhere whose flag you'd recognise
or ever fly. And it will all be time limited
and tidy. And over,

bar the roaring, by the time
the literary industrial complex
concludes its search for what rhymes (or almost)
with Lockheed's, Northrop's, and General Dynamics'
sky-scraping share price.

The meadow's been built over.
And I've buttoned back up.

iii.
Things You Should Know About Higgins

Exclusivity Principle

You aren't fully alive
until Death pings your doorbell
and asks for someone else.

You cannot know you are truly good
without the continued existence of the names
in the jailed socialite's black book.

The laughter thrown by a visit from an old friend is made
all the bigger by the house across the road
loud with the sound of nobody today
nobody tomorrow.

You can't be sure your life is useful
without the knowledge
certain newspaper columnists
are still somewhere
breathing air.

No journey of self discovery is complete
until it takes you past
an ex-bicycle wedged in a winter canal.

My Becoming

The boy whose favourite music
used to be the theme tune from Black Beauty,
within five years, forms the considered opinion
the world would be much improved
if certain people had their throats slit.
I am ten years old
and watching *Roots*, been introduced
to the memorably dressed gentlemen
of the Ku Klux Klan.

Don't play with that Traveller boy.
His name: Thomas Sweeney.
But people like him don't matter
to the sort of people
I'm supposed to grow up to be.
Eventually, as is the way of children
I never see him again.
I am nearly eleven.

Ever since,
though I try to be good,
whenever I hear
a mouthful of excellent teeth
not quite rhyme *democracy*
with *decent hard working majority*,
or a decent hard working
tobacco hands gom
spit *people like them
no respect*

I want to bestow
on just one such spitter
or set of politically astute teeth, the gift
of waking up with their throat slit.
Fifty six next birthday.
And I still listen out for
the theme from Black Beauty
but hardly ever hear it.

The Panic of July 1980

My Mother started doing Bed and Breakfast
and in a panic before the first guests
got her curtains cleaned
at the Magdalene Laundry.

She wasn't over religious
and never joined the Nazi Party
or voted for Dana
except, perhaps, by accident.

She wasn't in favour of slavery,
except that particular day
when in a sweat
before the first guests
she needed a slave –
though no one called it by that name –
to do some of the sweating for her.

Unlike so many others,
we never joined the Nazi Party
or ate our dinner
on the backs of forced labourers.
Except one panicky afternoon
in the summer of 1980
when no one called it by that name.

St Jude's

That house, I have slept in every room,
bar kitchen and bathroom,
even the sitting room.
But now it is otherwise.

In that house, I thought I would go to Hell;
and, later, that I had already checked in there.
Though that was only the beginning.

In that house, things we must never mention.
Though in the privacy of our own minds
we speak of little else.

In that house, God finally went away.

In that house, a teenager forever
breaking a plate across a tiled floor
with his Sunday dinner still on it.

Being Nobody

I did it once, for a year, and loved it.
I was the nobody who moved into
the flat upstairs from you;
the nobody beside you
in the post office queue;
the nobody buying a cooked chicken
in the Monday morning supermarket
which he'll later share with nobody.

If anyone knocked,
I shouted from my rocking chair
that there was nobody here,
and it was always true.

I threw parties
and invited nobody
and they always turned up.

I was on nobody's mailing list,
not even the International Association of Nobodies.

Today I'm downloading the application form
you fill in
when you want to be
nobody again,
am no longer able
for all this
being somebody.

On Being Even Slightly Well Known

Those hours when the sun is away sulking
on beaches in Australia, Cape Town, Rio
and the storm rattling the window
shakes me awake,
I am everyone I have ever
allegedly been:
things I said in a cafe 20 years ago,
things I definititely didn't say...

According to one woman on the Internet
I should be dropped
without a parachute
out of an airplane
after, presumably, it's taken off
and cruising, ladies and gentlemen,
at forty thousand feet.
Thing is, I don't like heights.

Whenever I stoop
to read the comments section
I become my detractors,
find myself
sometimes even
agreeing with them.

Being known is like being dead.
You belong to them.

You Only Know Someone

By how strategically they kiss
all the bits and make it look indiscriminate

By how, their mouth gone beaky,
drops what it has no further need to kiss

By how they laugh at your jokes
as if you're running some type of
friendly electricity through them

By the jokes they strategically decide
to stop laughing at, instead twitch like a slightly
disapproving member of an interview panel
which of course is what they'll end up being

By who they stoop to discreetly vomit on

By measuring them in absolute inverse proportion
to how great you remember
them telling you
you are

From a certain angle, he is you

He arrived from nowhere
and will, we expect, soon be going back there.
Of late he sits outside the bookstore on Central Avenue,
the sort of place that, these days, specialises
in selling books about Russia
to skinny accountants with stutters
and rotund autodidacts who dream
mostly of the next cream cake.
The town paces past him in a rush
to purchase various types of insurance
or get their wedding rings resized.

From a certain angle
he is you
thirty years ago,
as he rocks
in perfect time to a song
only he can hear.
After dark, he likely goes to a room
for which forms have been filled out
and a box each night is ticked.

When I glance at him I realise
he's alive
and you're not.
You're dead, by your own hand.

The question here is less
what went wrong
than what went right,
for sometimes he
is what things going right looks like.

Memorial to Myself

I have been away toasting tables lined
with the pricier variety of imbecile;
humouring old buzzards in Aran sweaters
and cranky caps
until their sweaters collapsed
threadbare off their bastard backs.
I have cut ribbons for guys
floating balloons across the town square
and calling it dance.
I have eaten with people of enormous importance
and forgotten most of their names.

I did not shrivel like the rest of them.
Though they thought they had me
I was not bought and sold at the market stall
where you can get (third hand)
Fianna Fail senators cheaper
than Mayo flags two weeks after
an All Ireland defeat.

I am again what I was before
and secretly always was
though I sometimes had to hide it.
I did not kill the dream I dreamt with those others
not all of whom made it this far.
Tonight I consult their ghosts.

What I Am Not

after Eugenio Montale

I'm not one of those people
who takes his tea or his politics decaf
or with artificial sweetener.
I'm a feminist, if you'll forgive
the genitalia, but not
the sort who invites Peter Sutcliffe
to read from his memoir
at their literary festival
because he promised
to favourably review her next novel
in Hustler magazine,
then tearfully denounces him on Twitter
when she remembers
how he carved up all those women.
That, Sister, would be you.
Not the sort who joins you
and your two most expensive aunties
for cream-tea in the good room
while there's still the possibility
of eating mouldy cheese sandwiches
down the butt of the bus
with nobody you'd want to meet.

Not the sort of person who gives
an easy yes or no to anything
when there's still the chance
to whisper maybe to everything

except the applicant
with the matching jaw and jacket.

Status Update at 55 ¼

I am not yet officially it.
No university has thus far
put a silly hat on my head
to honour my contribution.
I have never made top item
on the Nine O'Clock News;
but apart from the sex scandal which did,
I'm probably the best known boy of my year.
I was recently translated into Russian,
have been called "much loved",
"famous", "the Rambo of Irish poetry",
and, if you scavenge the internet, far worse than that.
Just when I think the world's forgotten my name,
someone says it again.

But inside the man with the name
much uttered, typed, and spat
still the boy who moved house
six times in nine years and was always
new to whatever street.
All the evenings I had to concede
the impossibility of playing
table tennis against myself;
that a game of solitary soccer
can still be lost.
The back garden wall sometimes
harder to beat than Leeds Utd with Lorimer,
Norman bites-yer-legs, and Giles
for boys no one wants to know.

Things You Should Know About Higgins

after Claes Andersson

Higgins is not surprised to hear his name is Viking;
that his origins are people who were big into pillage
and the thing that usually goes with pillage.

Higgins sometimes tells those who ask
if they're related, that the President
is his illegitimate father.

Higgins visits Czechoslovakia
in his dreams. Usually while he's awake.

If Higgins had business cards,
they would say "poet and hitman".
Higgins looks forward to one day
actually killing someone.

Higgins isn't exactly joking.

When Higgins says: "You think so?"
the conversation is over.

Higgins can't drive.
Higgins can't swim.
But apart from that Higgins
knows everything.

Higgins never repeats himself, except
always.

Higgins disagrees. Most of the time.
Especially with himself.

Higgins isn't planning to get a new kitchen.
Ever. But suggest away.

Higgins secretly thinks
the old wallpaper
should be reinstalled.

Higgins wants for Christmas
a long leather coat,
the sort interrogators used to wear
in what Higgins calls: "the good old days".

Higgins thinks you're just jealous.

Higgins feeds stray cats
slices of ham out the back window
when none of the family is watching,
in the hope they might come back.
They do. Same time every night.
And then one night they don't.

My RSVP

This invitation that I apply –
online, naturally –
for membership of that thing
that calls itself society;
first perfect the art of nodding gravely
while nibbling blue cheese –
or what they say is blue cheese –
on some sort of biscuit;
then slowly die hoping
to be crowned one day for the newspapers –
the sun hanging above me
like a runny fried egg –
with an honorary doctorate
in saying fuck you politely;

their latest ruse to manoeuvre
me away from me
and into their world
so they can measure me
and force on me
something I already knew:
that from their point of view
I am never a good idea.

The Social Whirl

These days we attend more
hospital appointments than parties.
You show me your irregular cells.
I fondle my swollen lymph node and note
it's grown more that the world economy last month.
It's either Death setting up that trophy clinching goal
or my immune system being the guy
who stands middle of the road
on an otherwise quiet Sunday
shouting at imaginary traffic.
Your digestive system is the lady on the internet
who makes everything about transsexuals.
The big debate: whether either of us
has the right change to get a bag of
highly questionable crisps,
some doubtful Maltesers,
or an ill-advised orange drink
from the waiting room machine.
For these days we attend more
hospital appointments than parties.

Instead of sliding you and my new hair cut
across the floor almost stylishly
at the sort of party disgraced
former ambassadors to China
attend when trying to get back into society,
shuffling across my own kitchen
I invent a new dance:
the Kevin Higgins limp.
Then waltz my lungs upstairs
for another extended siesta
zipped into their trainee body bag
where they'll await
the next hospital appointment
and the appointment after that.

A Kind of Love

after U. A. Fanthorpe

There is a kind of love called forbearance
which doesn't run screeching
permanently down the street
days you go about the place
wearing what she knows are
the wrong glasses, and your arse
isn't where you left it, so she again
has to point you in its general direction;

which doesn't mind as much as it should
when, trying to bleed
the upstairs radiator, you instead
start it blubbering
black water all night into
her only free basin, because it's Christmas Eve
and there isn't a plumber;

which appears to instantly forgive
when next day you by accident
refreeze part of the turkey and so now stand
madly defrosting said bird with her hairdryer
while she distracts herself peeling
the Brussels sprouts which only you'll eat;

which doesn't fasten you into
a motorised high chair, as most would,
when she finds several tiny pieces
of the ham only you eat
under the settee;

which – though that golden five minutes
during which it was hoped
you might say something witty
are clearly long past – restrains the cat
when he suggests she discreetly
take you to the vet for the injection from which
none come around;

which puts up with you
even when you've a look on you as if
you haven't had a good poo since
the National Organisation of Labour Students
Conference nineteen ninety two,
about which she knows you'll soon
insist on telling her again;

the kind of love which makes sure
you come home from work
to a light left on for you
over the front door
winter nights.

Friday, November 18th, 2022

Peace came in the door
and sat down beside me
and said how glad it was to see me,
genuinely, and to finally meet my wife.
I knew I must take its hand
though I did not know who I would be
in the absence of all I had built
its belligerent opposite into.

Peace came in the door
and introduced itself to us
I did not know its face
my high wall against it
had served longer
than anyone in Long Kesh –
twenty seven years –
and bore much graffiti
but I knew the name it told me was true
and I had to take its hand.

A much smaller man than I remember
and so, I realised, now was I
the day Peace sat down among us
and said it went by my father's name.

Disappointment

after Ernst Bloch

Every saint loses their halo
in learning to walk on Earth,
every hope its aura
in coming to life.

Overthrow
with your tiny insistent why
any gold or silver plated
gods who block your way.

Be everything you wish,
especially that for which
you don't have permission.

And embrace disappointment
as the necessary shortfall
of the wished for thing
becoming itself.

Make the world
rather than be made by it.

Acknowledgements

The editor and publishers wish to acknowledge the many journals, magazines and newspapers which have published individual poems from this collection. Likewise, thanks are due to the radio stations and podcasts who broadcast work from this volume. We are unable to provide an exhaustive list of same; however, your support meant a lot to Kevin as well as to us.

"Mr Cogito Considers The Side Effects" was chosen by Saolta Arts' Poems for Patience Project, 2023, to appear framed on a wall in University Hospital, Galway.

"Temple of Electricity" appears in the 2025 anthology *We Are All Palestinians*, published by Culture Matters, UK. Profits from the anthology will benefit Medical Aid for Palestinians.

KEVIN HIGGINS was co-organiser of Over The Edge literary events in Galway for twenty years, from 2003 until his death in 2023. He published six previous full collections of poems: *The Boy With No Face* (2005), *Time Gentlemen, Please* (2008), *Frightening New Furniture* (2010), *The Ghost In The Lobby* (2014), *Sex and Death at Merlin Park Hospital* (2019), and *Ecstatic* (2022), all with Salmon Poetry. His poems also featured in *Identity Parade: New British and Irish Poets* (Bloodaxe, 2010) and in *The Hundred Years' War: modern war poems* (Ed Neil Astley, Bloodaxe May 2014). Kevin was satirist-in-residence with the alternative literature website The Bogman's Cannon from 2015 to 2016. *2016 – The Selected Satires of Kevin Higgins* was published by NuaScéalta in 2016. *The Minister For Poetry Has Decreed* was published by Culture Matters (UK) also in 2016. *Song of Songs 2:0: New & Selected Poems* was published by Salmon in Spring 2017. Kevin was a highly experienced workshop facilitator and several of his students have gone on to achieve publication success. He facilitated poetry workshops at Galway Arts Centre and taught Creative Writing at Galway Technical Institute for fifteen years. Kevin was the Creative Writing Director for the NUI Galway International Summer School and also taught on the NUIG BA Creative Writing Connect programme. His poems have been praised by, among others, Tony Blair's biographer John Rentoul, *Observer* columnist Nick Cohen, writer and activist Eamonn McCann, historian Ruth Dudley Edwards, and *Sunday Independent* columnist Gene Kerrigan; and have been quoted in *The Daily Telegraph*, *The Independent*, *The Times* (London), *Hot Press* magazine, *The Daily Mirror* and on The Vincent Browne Show, and read aloud by Ken Loach at a political meeting in London. He published topical political poems in publications as various as *The New European*, *The Morning Star*, *Dissent Magazine* (USA), *Village Magazine* (Ireland), & *Harry's Place*. *The Stinging Fly* magazine has described Kevin as "likely the most widely read living poet in Ireland". One of Kevin's poems features in *A Galway Epiphany*, the final instalment of Ken Bruen's Jack Taylor series of novels. His work has been broadcast on RTE Radio, Lyric FM, and BBC Radio 4. He was a regular contributor to the podcast *Not the Andrew Marr Show*, hosted by Crispin Flintoff; its audience posthumously voted Kevin a Labour Hero of 2023. *Mentioning the War*, a collection of his reviews and essays, was published by Salmon in 2012. His book *The Colour Yellow & The Number 19: Negative Thoughts That Helped One Man Mostly Retain His Sanity During 2020* was published in late 2020 by Nuascealta. His extended essay 'Thrills & Difficulties: Being A Marxist Poet In 21st Century Ireland' was published in pamphlet form by Beir Bua Press in 2021. *Life Itself* is published posthumously.

IRISH FICTION
Cúirt
International
Festival of Literature

salmonpoetry
Cliffs of Moher, County Clare, Ireland

"Publishing the finest Irish and international literature."
Michael D. Higgins, President of Ireland